THE BLACKLINES SCRAWL

THE BLACKLINES SCRAWL

BY STANLEY H. BARKAN

Commemorative Chapbook

Yugoslavia
Struga Poetry Evenings

Italy
Sicilian Antigruppo

Cross-Cultural Communications
Merrick, New York
2004

Acknowledgment is made, with thanks, to the editors of the fol-lowing newspapers, magazines, and anthologies in which the poems in this volume first appeared:

Bitter root
Dodeca
El Verano (Mexico)
High Points
Poet Lore
Shantih
The Human Voice Quarterly
The National Poetry Anthology
The Washington Square Journal
The Washington Square Review
The Writer
Trapani Nuova (Sicily)

Special thanks to David B. Axelrod, Tihomir Kondev, Miloje Popović, and Saverio A. Scammacca for their advice and efforts in making possible this commemorative chapbook.

Published by
Cross-Cultural Communications
239 Wynsum Avenue, Merrick, NY 11566-4725
Tel: (516) 868-5635. Fax: (516) 379-1901
E-mail: cccpoetry@aol.com
www.cross-culturalcommunications.com

ISBN 0-89304-010-X Paperback
ISBN 0-89304-016-9 Hardcover

Designed and illustrated by Bebe Barkaı
Reprinted in Bulgaria

CONTENTS

For Bebe

and our best creations,

Mia and Scotty

LINES

The blacklines scrawl
along the corners of the night
tracing corridors in the caverned stillness—
graphs of grey shades to sable.

The reddened sun peers rays in umbered edges
waking the dark-light of evening's morning.

I'll slide my pen along the lane of my slant vision
and touch the colors vertical, outside ...

But for the moment
I mark the stillness
with you alone
in a peopleless city.

NANTUCKET

The cobbled quickness
   veering and tacking
     down
       and round
  evenless bikepaths ...

      The whale teeth and
      darjeeling tea
        mingle with the tarpaulins,
         nets, and salt currents
          of crusted air ...

    The fog
   sounds horns
to blow the ships
        that drifted out for
   worldly quests ...

    The spermacetti pots
    are boiling and the
      scent exudes ...

A lone and tattered beach
  where polyphemi dessicate ...

   Touches of long-dead
    ambergris
      and duffels dragged
  in the sand ...

... while you and I ride
       the thin
   wires
    rounded

And pause awhile
in pequod thoughts,
gam amid the hemp,
harpoons, and quadrant views,

... and sail the world for inner
      Moby Dicks.

LA PLAGE PUBLIQUE

Yellow-blue and blue-and-white
Parasols spread, stuck in sand ...
Bikinis yellow-green and green-and-bright,
Bronzed and browned and yellow-tanned ...
La Plage Publique.

A light-blue saucer sky,
Lemon sun with rays awry ...
Transistors blaring,
Bespectacled noses leering ...
La Plage Publique.

Orange rinds and banjoes plucked,
Towels spread,
Yellow-red
Rippled winds—gently ducked ...
La Plage Publique.

The sails are floating,
everyone's boating,
while I am noting ...
La Plage Publique.

THE SONG OF THE DULZAINA

I have heard the Dulzaina with its double reeds
Trill sonorous tunes,
And I have seen carved necklaces of stone with unmatched beads
Lie like cast cryptic runes—
But still I am not moved ...
I cannot think what has been proved.

And I have smelled the red carnations
With their candy taste.
And eaten Bouillabaisse fit for oblations,
Half of which went to waste—
But still I am not moved ...
I cannot think what has been proved.

And I have touched the warm-ivory skin
Of statues come to life,
And moved with Kali rhythm to hands soft with sin—
Sinuous hands, in each a knife—
But still I am not moved ...
I cannot think what has been proved.

And now I'm in the Alhambran garden
With cascading blossoms red and white,
And sit upon ground which cannot harden
In the grove of cypresses against the night—
And I am moved ...
I need not know what has been proved.

THE MUMMIES OF GUANAJUATO

These are the tombs where the mummies lie,
Here in the tunnels of the dark inside.
The natives knew they'd not take long to die,
See how they struggled, their mouths stretched wide.

Some, mother and child together, died in birth;
Others of ills the cause or cure not known.
They cut out these deep square blocks of earth,
And marked each one with a dated stone.

Like wooden monuments they now stand:
One on his knees as if he wished to pray;
Another with a cross closed in his hand,
With little sign of bodily decay.

They are doomed to writhe eternally,
Locked in flesh in a breathless agony.

A HOUSE OF DEMONS

The glass madonna
stains its light upon
the flickering pews

beneath the hanging tapers
where sit the saintly gargoyles
robed in cerements of wax

nostrils quivering from
the stale wafers
pasted on their tongues:

translucent miracles.

O, Lord, why do you congregate
yourself in a house of demons?

INSECT LOVE

My eyes
crawl over
the flesh of my love
quivering with delight

The brush
of our legs
makes locust rhythms
in the night of candles
drawing us to their flame

We blaze
against the waxen stake
melted into semen ash

Then rise
phoenix moths
seeking for the light.

WAITING

It's hot not only in Montana
(And not only in the afternoon—
Unless you mean long after noon), Mr. Eli Siegel,
But here in the lounge of the city college
With the sun streaking hotly on my open-collared neck.

I sit hot, waiting, in-between time.
I'd like to coolly glide my pen without a rhyme—
But the old corridors keep me in place ...
And the sun sweats on my wrinkled ears.

It's hot, after a while with songs and summers,
Hot in late, late noon—
Soon the white night will
Spill down on the stairs
And lift me from my pen and book.

I'll turn the page
And shift my seat—
But O, the sun's streaks,
Hot upon my neck ...
I cannot move.

The yellow heat holds me—
Crumpled in my chair—
Late in-transit time,
Worn from sleep and talk and worried looks.

The books upon the
Shelves, all shifted "out of joint,"
Wait for a groping finger
And a caressing palm,
And eyes, O, eyes
Streaking down upon
The waiting pages
Hot in the late, late
After noon in city college hall.

THE DREAMERS

You speak to me of rhymes,
The past, and glorifying times.
I nod my head
And wonder when you'll come to bed.

You lift your arm and cigarette
And breathe out from your nose.
You run your tongue along your lips
And make them wet.

I trace my fingers, just their tips,
Along the ridges of your spine
And linger in the line
Between your thigh and hips.

A little wine sits in the glass
Half off and on the chair,
And ashes spill upon the grass
Of carpet we bought last year.

You speak to me of rhymes
And turn your head.
I roll to my side of the bed
And dream of glorifying times
... of black olives and red wines.

IN ANOTHER TOWN

In another town
I would seek you

but you wouldn't come,
we wouldn't meet

I would search for you in the eyes
glinting in the streetlamps

their halos mocking,
your smile their penumbra

At coffee tables
I would sit staring

into the bottom of my cup
for patterns in the coffee grounds—

for Tarot forms in the forks and knives
for black mirrors in the convex spoons

And through the window
the mannequin forms

reflect the emblems
of our broken lives.

In another town
I would seek you,

but here I find you
in the shattered glass.

CHELSEA NIGHT

I
You, Lautrec woman,
pasteled on the tablecloth
in the cellar cafe
reading poems

the green absinthe light
casting shadows
on face and hair,
black snakes toothing the air
between puffs of cigarettes
and coffee sips

The stir of arsenic spoons
in cracked cups,
papers shuffled in your hand
circled by long candle faces
chiaroscuroed on the walls

Puppet strings
pasted on
a voice in motion.

II
We wandered
down that Chelsea street

seeking a place
in the alleyways

away from
city lamps

hiding from the moon
and unshaded windows

a place where
no stars dwell

Only where
your eyes

could light
my night.

IV
Standing by the window
to the city,
all the lamps burning
mirroring the sheets,
towels, bedclothes
strewn about the room

we're framed,
dimensioned as are
the buildings

focusing our
past and future lives.

Is this where Dylan
broke flasks of Welsh,
bursts of glass fury,

the wild maidens
sang a chorus
to his green and easy loves?

Is this where
all the fierce poets
came like roaches
out of the walls,
patterning their rimes,
their rimeless motions
on the pillows
of this amber
Chelsea night?

VI
You ignite small
novae in the ganglia
of my mesof lesh.

IX
My snowf lesh melts
          into your burning earthworks ...
You are fire, I ice.

X
I cannot feel
the sun anymore.

The wind does nothing
to my skin.

My feet kick stones
But only the stones are moved.

The scream of gulls
starts swimmers from the beach
but I am still.

Only the long fingers
of a Chelsea night.

XI
On the back
of old envelopes
on windowsills
and doors
on fences
on bricks in alleyways
I'll write my love
of you.

XII
I write my poems
on the inside of my skin

Incise them on underside
of palms, of breasts, of eyes.

I am all poem
all words and metaphor.

My fingers are all quills
scratching graffiti odes of you.

I will scribe no more,
your form is poem enough for me.

XV
I did not know
why Vincent cut
his ear

went mad under
the sky of Provence.

I did not know
why he sought
to merge his brush
with his blood

his eyes
with rainbows
of the field

with sunflowers,
        sunlight,
        sun ...

I did not know
until I dissolved
in you.

XVII
I'm angry at the table
between us—
the forks, the cups,
the knives.

I'm furious at the clock,
the stop lights,
wires of phones,
and working hours

At the failure
of flesh to merge,
of atoms to join.

O, if I cannot in you
dissolve,
we are separate
forever.

XVIII
I pick up the phone
to hear your voice,
thinking I heard
it ring

Your voice buzzing
in my brain.

But you do not call,
only the recorded sound
breaks the wired monotone
Hum-m-m-m-m-m-m-m-m-m

You were "gone"
when I called,
when I sought
the caresses of your tone

And now I'm deaf for you—
O give me back the gift of sound.

XIX
The morning eggs
        are lies,
The toast is just
        a fake.

Then why does
the clock say,
"Never, never, never ...?"

XX
Etched into my soul
is only one Chelsea night.

XXI
Perhaps love is only
as long as a single Chelsea night.

23

THE STATUE OF LIBERTY
"I see that you, too, build monuments,
to your great dead." — G. B. Shaw

And like Lazarus,
the Statue of Liberty
rises out of the river
speaking Emma's poem:

"Oh, you tired, you huddled masses,
yearning to breathe smog!"

And the fog girdles round her,
out of the refuse of 8,000,000 +
Americans.

"America, the Beautiful ...?"

This the sister
of the blind justice
with scales imbalanced.

Oh, if she'd tear the cloth
from her eyes,
then, too, like Oedipus,
tear the eyes as well,
to soothe them from the air ...
to hide them from the sewer
rats swimming round her feet.

And Egalité, the little sister,
holds high her little torch
on the Île de Cité,
waving in French semaphore
the wishes of her trinity—
Oh, Liberté, Egalité, Fraternité—
Oh, Citizen, Comrade, Brother.

History *à trois*
        na troikh?

And Emma Bovary and Emma Lazarus
join smog lights across the world.

Below her feet,
in the pedestal, surface deep,
the dungeons with their shackles creep,
and we peep
about and seek to insinuate ourselves,
to reach the Crown of Thorns.

Oh, the smile, that Gioconda smile,
and all the while
the *Ner Tamid*
flickers in the Roentgen air.

The bad air
above the fishes of the Fisherman
staring with their monocular eyes,
staring, looking for skies,
walking on the water
of the butt-end of our lives.

And still the Pequod
seeks to sail to sea
with Ahab forever plunging
his thrice-dipped harpoon into the greying whale.

And the monomaniacal eye
of the Mariner
stares his Ancient stare

joining Raskolnikov
and the yellow-eyed bird
upon the bust of Pallas.

And the *yetzer ha-ra* (the bad inclination)
and the *yetzer ha-tov* (the good inclination)
vied with one another.

Still stand the stones
above the gamma-shrouded air.

Still shines the Empire's
lamp to lighthouse.

And the Grand Inquisitor
came again, walking upon
the fish-strewn water,
staring into the widened eyes
of our Sacred American Lady.

"You would I melt in the melting pot.
You would I grind to Auschwitz burgers.
Now lift your arm beside
the brassy door
of the Golden Gate
and the bridges
joining."

As Marx and Freud and Einstein
dance their Hasidic dance
thrice around the metal maypole
of Our Lady
with dollars, sex, and atoms
woven in her hair.

Oh, Ozymandias,
look on *my* works
and despair.

And Teiresias
saw his visions
and the Shaman
sang his songs
and the town drunks
told the true stories of The Old West.

Now all carved, preserved, in graffiti patterns
on the greying folds
of our monument to ...
our mausoleum of ...
Freedom.

STREETLAMPS

Her marquee smiles—

Streetlamps gawking
in the alleyways

where blind cats
rummage in the dark.

Mirror eyes
reflect the souls
of passers-by

flashing in the neon smoke,

green cigarettes
in their glowing mouths.

Only the mannequin windows
mock her painted hips.

NOLI ME TANGERE

I would be more tender
than the tenderest lover
to you the sharer of my wild compare,

to you who'd bathe me with your hands
as I do you with words.

I would put no limit,
no cutting point
to this my combined love,
but you say, *"Noli me tangere!"*

How can I "touch you not"
when there is but *one* sense?
We touch with word and eye and mouth.

We cannot be without touching.
Can the wind blow without touching?
Do sounds upon our ears, our skin,
our minds impinge without touch?

I'd rather the snow would never fall
than touch you "only once."

In the snowless world,
there is no once
but only "ever."

Never is better
than not to love freely,

unpatterned as a storm,
unsevering as the waves,
unlimited as the wind.

Touch me not
for I am rimeless motion
born of primal flame.

Noli me *tangere.*

THE BOOK OF DREAMS

The comet, Kohoutek, writes
a warning on the wall of sky.

O, my Kamala,
shall we feast with Belshazzar
to the end of days?

Shall I kneel to you to tunes
of the sackbut and psaltery?

O, beware the fiery furnace,
for I am Daniel
come to tell your visions.

I will not bow but to the East.
In the Book of Dreams
do I sleep
and read:
MENE, MENE, TEKEL, UPHARSIN!

Will you heed
the beast upon the beach of Babylon,

Eat the stolen fruits,
dare to walk into
the den of beasts,
O, my beloved?

WOMAN OF MANHATTAN

O, woman of Manhattan,
you are my Kamala.

You teach me of olives
and cool wine.

You bathe my eyes
with musk and tamarind.

Your hands are the flow
of waves and warm wind.

Your voice, the lure
of a thousand streetlamps.

I follow in your wake,
slaked by your white smile.

EAST OF THE LAND OF NOD

My soul a Cezanne cube
   through which no light
      can pass

No dark or broken shadows
   flickering on wall
      or wind

Stained with the blood of leaves
   torn from spirit forms
      wailing.

No mark or circled lines
   spiraling up the gyre
      of flame

Infernoed by the split of eyes
   ripped out of sight
      and mind

Beyond the guarded gate
   sword ing the way
      to trees

Swollen with bitter apples
   gorged by sly worms
      waiting.

GEMINI WOMAN

Oh, Gemini woman,
twin demon lover.

Are you succubus or Lilith
come to steal or serve my nights?

Between the flames
of skin and soul, I wait.

Cooled and burned
wrestling with your form.

In the seventh house
of fire and water

Hurling through Limbo
with Paolo and Francesca

Wailing at a mouth
of honeydew and milk

I tell the twice-told tale
of Paradise and Hell.

NAYMAN

Let me say nay
to all patterns
linking birth to death,
sleep to a thousandth life.

Let me say nay
to the scissors of the clock
cutting to sunder
at a second's stroke.

Let me say nay
to her who'd mark me
in her book of hours,
unman me in some fashioned place
without grass,
without the blinding sun
to burn my loins
alive.

Let me say nay
to the return of comets,
the fixed turn of sky;
hold back the waving
flurry of the spray,
the cyclic fall of leaves
and burst of seeds.

Let me say nay
to my old foe
I wrestle with
from cock's crow
to knell of bell
clappering at the croak
of sun
and quartering
of the madman moon.

Let me say nay
to the scythy
slicing of the days,
take his grinning skull
and split him up a tree,
duel with the guarding sword,
walk through the fire unscorched
and over the ice stretch
from Eden to the end of days
and blast the phoenix
back to flight.

ALWAYS, ALWAYS

Always, always
the dark nightmare
of your revel
in the hairy forests
of hot-house men
haunts my naked thoughts

Flashings between the glowing flies.
What do they need light for?
What do they seek
in the deep grass,
the fallen flowers,
the rotted roots?

Moonburned I turn
away from sky
bright with too many stars,
too few clouds
to shade away the laser truth
of fixed beacon warnings.
Always, always

GONE

Gone
She's gone.
And I live
But cannot breathe.
Left without a mouth
Untongued by her goodbye.
Blind, deaf—stopped of all sense!
No face to launch my thousand ships,
No fingers to find my furrowed brow,
No voice to speak my name out of Limbo.
Now, who will say to me, "Rise up, Lazarus!"
Who will make that descent, the deep-spiraled journey
Guide me out of the cave across the burning river
Through the long flames where I may breathe again her breathless kiss.

WHEN LOVE FALLS

When love falls
from your fingers
like an old newspaper
wasting on the sidewalk,
kicked by passers-by,
splattered in the manholed gutters,
torn for street-dwellers' tissue,
blown across the asphalt corners,
gathered for park-people's soles
keeping off the grass
where chess players
gambit between the squares
dreaming of stalemates
on last year's page 72,

I will write
my tabloid pain
upon the tables
waiting for the rain
to wash away
the ink of queens
... and drown.

SILENT DARK

When even the early sundreams
are shrouded behind
impenetrable clouds,
the starless nights endure
and morning
comes without a light,
like blindmen
we will stumble through
the lampless streets,
beneath blackened windows
opened without eyes
to greet our opened mouths,
our seeking hands.
The white of teeth
cannot reflect
when even moons
are vanished from the sky.
We will listen
for a voice
that will not speak,
Shriek out
in the silent dark
for even an echo
to resound within
some hidden ear
muted in the stillness
of a world
etched into the grey
of forgetfulness.

AS STILL AS A BROOM

Love as still as a broom
leaning against a fireplace.

All the carpets swept,
all the ashes grated.

And the candles burned
down to the black wires.

And the windows frosted
starless, moonless.

No shoes under the bed,
no towel on the floor.

Only the crease in the pillow
and a smell I can't remember.

AFTER THE FALL

After the flood,
the raven and the dove
made nesting places
on the moon.

After the rain
came down,
the craters' manna
made igneous the earth

the seas gathered
into Sargasso mists
and albatrosses hung
from every neck
of corpses straddled
on the naked trees.

After the plowshares
turned to swords
slicing at the wind,
the mustard seeds
burst into flaming vines.

After the fall,
the ape man and Lilith
danced macabre
in the valley
of the dragon's teeth.

AS YET UNBORN

Oh to be Adam
again
with all his ribs
yearning for a woman
as yet unborn,
mouth free
of the taste of apples,
ears without
the hiss of snakes,
mindless of
nakedness and shame
in the garden
of gentle creatures
waiting for a name.

TO A BROOKLYN POET

(for Menke Katz)

Build me no monuments in Boro Park,
Statues for wild pigeons to decorate.
Let no one scurry through my attic
Nibbling bits and pieces of my life
Over the inkwells and the broken cups.
Just let my words live freely in the
Land of Manna, that third heaven where
Only children play, delighting in honey milk
Of the stars and mooncakes of the angels.
O Lord, let the insects sing my lyrics,
The worms feast on the flesh of my soul,
The furry beasts make selahs for each dawn.

HEKDESH

Seeking some crumbs
from the communal hekdesh,

My fingers find only
the ribbed spaces of the burlap,

Nothing even to catch
beneath my long talon nails.

Scraping around for bits
of old dough or broken crusts,

My hand gnaws the emptiness,
opening and closing like the beak

Of an ancient bird
crying for its lost young

(The days of nests and first flights
around the aging *shtetl*),

Seeking for a symbol or a sign
of seed to newly sprout

Out of the burnt-brown earth
into long wild wheat grass.

No smoke twirls out of this wind-torn hut,
no flames or even ashes in the rotting stove.

Where are the bakers
to make the fresh unleavened bread

That stales into the scraps
to fill this wasted beggar's bag?

ANGEL-CHILD

The tooth
under my pillow
will be stolen
by a mischievous
angel-child
He'll swap a coin
stamped: "The Land of Manna"
and I will listen
for the flapping
of the window shades
and rain mingling
with my wanderings
in the forty-wink desert.
I'll lie down in the oasis
and feast on dates,
halvah, and sesame seeds.
When Daddy wakes me,
I'll be his genie
and grant him wishes,
bite into his hand
with all my lost teeth
stolen away by the angel-child
to the third heaven
where only children play.

AIRMAIL TO THE SUN

I mail
my letter
with the 1936
stamp on it.
No address,
No name.
Perhaps the postman
will make some
wry remark
about new stamps
for old.
Maybe a genie
will rub out
between the watermark
and the postman's thumb.
He'll be marked *Airmail*
and promise wishes
and say: "Package me
and mail me to the sun."
There he will
ray down on me
with yellow ink
and find my lost address.
my deadletter name,
my old stamp book
protected from
the smoke of lamps,
in the morgues
where old letters never die.
There my letter
will open sesame
and, out of its envelope,
spill all of my
Aladdin longings.

SMELLS REMEMBERED

The smell of him
was like my son
clinging to me
in the late dawn—
out of troubled
sleep of Golems
throwing him over
the iron-gate balcony
down to the Zócalo
of our dining room.
The ashes in the fireplace—
where goblins
whisper, "Sally! Sally!"—
flicker with his
Rapid Eye Motion,
deepening his sleep.
And I remember
how *my* father woke
and, out of his sun-bright mouth,
said: "Crazy kid.
Go back to sleep!"
Selah.

DIPPING CAULIFLOWER

"It's raining," I said
as she went on
dipping torn bits of cauliflower
into the thousand-island dressing.

She agreed,
nodded her head,
and continued munching
the pink-&-white florets.

And so did I
with drops of water
spotting the round redwood
umbrella-less picnic table
in the backyard,
sitting on one of the two benches
between the plastic
green-&-aluminum beach chairs,

reading *Fruits & Vegetables*
and writing about the undigested bits of words
stuck between my teeth,
watching the ink
blot on the blank spots
between the print
on the pages
      & pages
      of prose
      & poetry
by someone like her
for someone like me.

Then she picked up
the plate & the bowl,
opened the screen door,
and vanished into the kitchen.

And I stayed
salad-less, outside,
waiting for the rain
to wash me out
of my place on the bench,

and put my pen
back into my torn pocket
from whence it came.

ZERO

Zero is a scream
without sound

without time,
without space.

I wait ...
am placed
upon a plate
for open mouths
to take into their silences.

I am zero—
Let me be heard!